The Arrival

The Arrival

Daniel Simko

Edited by Carolyn Forché and James Reidel

Four Way Books
Tribeca

Editorial Office
Four Way Books
POB 535, Village Station
New York, NY 10014
www.fourwaybooks.com

Library of Congress Cataloging-in-Publication Data
Simko, Daniel.
The arrival / Daniel Simko ; edited by Carolyn Forché and James Reidel.
p. cm. -- (A Stahlecker series selection)
ISBN 978-1-884800-92-4 (pbk. : acid-free paper)
I. Forché, Carolyn. II. Reidel, James. III. Title.
PR9170.S563S56 2009
821'.92--dc22
2009004716
ISBN: 978-1-884800-92-4

This book is manufactured in the United States of America
and printed on acid-free paper.

Four Way Books is a not-for-profit literary press. We are grateful for the
assistance we receive from individual donors, public arts agencies,
and private foundations.

This publication is made possible with public funds
from the National Endowment for the Arts
and from the New York State Council on the Arts, a state agency.

Distributed by University Press of New England
One Court Street, Lebanon, NH 03766

We are a proud member of the Council of Literary Magazines and Presses.

[clmp]

NATIONAL
ENDOWMENT
FOR THE ARTS
A great nation
deserves great art

CONTENTS

II Fragments & Abandoned Verse

INTRODUCTION

This, Svetozar Daniel Simko's first book of poetry in America, is also his last, so *The Arrival* is at once a book of presence and absence, the shimmering debut of a lyric poet whose reticence kept him from a wider audience during his life—and it is at the same time the quiet culmination of his life's work. In the beginning, there is a "Departure," a taking leave that marks these poems with itinerancy and loss: a changed address, and then later *the living with someone who is not there*, and a dwelling in *solitude in place of a body*. This is a voice hovering between worlds and languages, spiritually suspended above its dread, but also tethered to wakeful hope and poignant love, no matter how elusive. That this love transcended the circumstances of his life is a tribute to him, and to the power of lyric utterance.

"Note Left on a Table" is among these love poems, taking the form, as its title suggests, of a note left for an absent beloved, a belated address alluding to an argument, to sex and gardens, falling water and flight. The poem's repetitions hint of frustrated attempts at explanation and a desire for clarity, but this is not a book of love poems as commonly understood. It is, rather, a *score for voice* in a libretto of exile and survival, at once of the historical moment and of a deep interiority of the human soul. Simko was considered an American poet, and was accomplished and comfortable in his adopted city of New York, but his soul had been tutored in Central Europe, and he was immersed in its literature and thought to a depth unimaginable by his American peers. So it is both sad and somewhat expected that his poems should appear in America posthumously, as this is love poetry for a childhood left behind when he arrived here from a city beside the Danube. *And if this is a poem of childhood,* he writes, *then it's also the darkness within the glove.*

First known in America as the translator of a critically acclaimed collection of the poetry of Georg Trakl, he shares with the Austrian a sense of past and present selves as severed, but for Simko the abandoned child of the past becomes a revenant, a figure of visitation, a companion from whom he cannot be separated by the passage of time. The event, in Simko's history, occurs on August 20, 1968, with the invasion of Czechoslovakia. *Writing back in code,* he writes, *the word for home is August.* His father remembers walking with his ten-year-old son through the occupied streets, shouting at the soldiers on their tanks. Eight months later, the family quietly departed for the United States, leaving their belongings behind in a relative's attic, whereupon the elder Simko became a professor at Cornell University in Ithaca, New York. To the leaflets on campus walls protesting the war in Vietnam and other causes, Daniel and his father added posters against the Soviet occupation of Czechoslovakia. On the first day of school, his father remembers, Daniel came home in tears, having been beaten by boys who did not understand his English. It was the beginning, perhaps, of the poet's obsession with speech and with giving voice to the past. *And yet,* he writes in the poem "A Field of Red Poppies," *this is a field / where they were throwing people once. // That's the story. // And it still matters. Because it is voiced.* Speech became for this poet a form of defiance, a means of breaking a collective and complicit silence wherein *memory is neglected, erased, wiped clean.* In many of his poems, the poet addresses himself, or, at times, the boy he had once been, who spoke *in the arrested voice you once used in a different language.* He laments: *I should have lain down in the mud / and listened to the tall elms speak my language.*

"I used to [bicycle with him] through the lush forests near the Danube bend where the wild garlic had a pervading smell," his father recently wrote, "…and through the corn fields on the outskirts of the town where the paths were strewn with wild poppies." In his son Daniel's poems, we find poplar and spruce, apple and pear trees, wild lilies and fields of poppies, which remind him of his childhood but also of *someone who is not there,* a self, perhaps, whom he is no longer.

The body, for the poet Simko, is replaced by solitude, and becomes a *pale ideogram* of itself, or *the flat light of a star,* or *a lost address,* that is, a place that cannot be found by the wandering soul. *It seems your address has changed,* he writes, *or not changed. Or changed again.* This is the poetry of exile and of exilic being: the past is irrecoverable, the present elusive, and the self so protean that it can never be grasped. *We went on living it in the lined paper given to us in childhood,* that is, living a life written into being. *Exile is a hard walk,* the poet admits, *an intricate tattoo,* an indelible mark, legible to those who perceive it. To those left behind, he writes *We have received letters and your kindness, / kisses, of course. // We have gone to hell.* This last phrase, a commonly used idiomatic epithet in English, is also very precisely deployed here to deflect any doubt as to the cost and true nature of a politically imposed itinerancy.

What seems to mark the absence of the body is its clothing, or more specifically, a white shirt as if waved before an enemy, surrendering to incorporeality, that can move *from one empty house to another* innocuously and without detection. In these poems the clothes are battered, or *blown into the fields.* The flesh becomes cloth and *at night your blood sleeps in your clothes.* This becomes interesting when one considers that an entire world can be contained for this poet within the darkness of a single lost glove. The past, of a country or an individual, can be read from its artifacts, from articles of clothing left behind, household objects tenderly beheld. The world is not obliterated, but remains legible, and this legibility becomes evidence of what occurred, and so the poet Simko retrieves from the ruins of what he has lost and left behind, a measure of hope for the preservation of historical memory and spiritual discernment.

We began with love and we will end with it, for the beloved appears throughout this work, an other so intensely perceived that her absence is itself cherished as *the same desire to go on living / with someone who is not there.* But desire it is, from a lover willing to endure longing *without anesthesia.* Whether nation or woman, the poet enters the beloved *the way an angel enters a scythe,* an image perhaps of erotic union, but one in which the disembodied soul submits to the harvest blade. It is a way of saying *yes* to everything, and with great tenderness. *I have come to love this city,* which I read as Bratislava, to which the poet returned for his first visit just after the liberation of 1989, *this one thing / I could not keep // The groves and vineyards that forgive me for leaving, / and the people who do not.* Perhaps, if the poet had lived, he would know that his poems were offered an afterlife both in his natal country and in his adopted America, and that for his departures from both he never need be forgiven. Adieu, Daniel, and may your poems touch hearts and endure.

—Carolyn Forché

I

DEPARTURES

I am already changing the address.

The one hung, pinned, or crucified against the wall, the one
        broken over a shrub.

But I am not afraid.

I am entering this room for the last time.

I am entering you the way an angel enters a scythe.

WINTER MUSIC

It has grown simpler.

It has grown into a map of hard fields,
the worry of a hand holding a knife.

It seems, after all,
that you have come to care for nothing.

Not even the voices rising into slow music
beneath the ice.

It seems that you have been occupying yourself
with nothing in particular.

It seems your address has changed,
or not changed. Or changed again.

Perhaps it is time to rise
and write it down:
                        the address, the phone number,
a clear description of your face—

Perhaps it is time to get dressed,
and step out into the blunt argument of the morning . . .

the same desire to go on living
with someone who is not there.

Cold light against your forehead,
solitude in place of a body.

HOMAGE TO GEORG TRAKL

In the bird-light, in the dream-light, messages
of the dead drift through windows.

What house is this? What grass?

Orion inbound, tattooed against the north wind.
Think of it.

Think of the last grievance,
the incomprehensible need to go on.

Perhaps now you can recall the pale ideogram of your
　　　　body,
which is the moon's,

rowing itself behind the clouds into past tense.

Or combing the hair of the dead,
as they lie, absolutely still,

as though someone was about to take their photograph.
And after all, this is why you came here.

This is why even apples fell into sin.

This bread, this wine, have silence
in their keeping.

This is how it begins.
Weaving the blood through the wrists of the damned.

This is how it continues:
The cold, the snow, the slight trembling in your hands.

One silent candle shines in the dark room.
A silver hand extinguishes it.

JANUARY

Hell bent blue moon, yellow eye of dust.
Cold irreparable desire.

I have been trying to explain something all night.
I am no longer sure of the subject.

St. George, the defender, freezes over.
There is still something I want to say, but not here.

I want to lie down with the snow.
I want the wild lilies to break their silence.

STILL LIFE: A TREATMENT

Vase, plate, picture, and cup:
places of darkness, places of kindness.
Clothes once touched hanging over a chair.

The frayed poplars, huge bodies of nothingness,
addressing the dark windows,
or the few avoiding the police.

But what's the use? Thousands of miles away
the Danube is a sketch of glass against the mined woods—
a face, a grape, a kernel.

I am writing your names down for the last time.
I am writing your names in secrecy.
Be silent . . . Be silent . . .

A peach glows reddish on the table.
A slice of apple falls into a glass of clear wine.
Whiteness is all. You are snow.

DEPOSITION

Yes, I know. It seems I have been talking a long time
without making much sense.

I have mentioned fists, and departures,
the dumb choreography of the blind.

Some invective, I suppose.
In the photograph, presented under dubious circumstances,

you appear to be waving,
I mean holding your hands up.

And that fist of ice, the knife-blade, and broken glass
are all a rude joke.

But of course you didn't know—
the dogs, the snow coming down on our bodies

which weigh nothing.
Which are grievances.

As for the address, there is none.
What was I saying?

All right. Continue.

FAR

Bells, coming in a mile off. The North Star reticent
against the Danube Bridge,
phrases falling on the cold metal.

The same bare poplar, the lonely spruce
weave in the late October wind.

Or as I imagine them now, looking at them from the promenade,
years younger,

the same mildly uncertain expression spreading over my face.

I have come to love this city, this one thing
I could not keep.

The groves and vineyards that forgive me for leaving,
and the people who do not.

And if this is a poem of childhood,
then it's also the darkness within a glove.

Or in a trumpet, that the man playing the circus all night
finally puts down.

He has been unable to push it out.

Until he turns into music.

CODA

All night you have been tearing maps in your sleep.
Your autobiography.

The crows rowing overhead are too silent to be crows.
The sky shows its overbite.

It must be raining.
There is no place to go but home.

AT 4 A.M.

So, what can you do with it all?

You can simply take it, and throw it against a wall.

You can pretend it's not there.

You are raising your hand to the page again.

You are signing a name which is not yours.

You are bending over the page.

All that is behind you now.

Still, it is impossible that you have been here.

It is in your file.

You could not be writing these lines to remember.

AGAINST OUR FORGETTING

I.

All night I thought of maps, grapes, and poppies,
the long road
stitched between the Danube and the oaks,

the insistence on travel cutting through our lives
like an issue
we were never comfortable with,
the argument flat, palm down, already lost.

But we went on living . . .
In the errant bee, in the mirror,
leaving hints
where we could find them,

moth-wing, bat-light, a journey home.

We went on living it in the lined paper
given to us in childhood,

where history, arriving with all its itinerant complaints
is only history, an insult, a bruise,

nagging for the exhaustion of light,
and movement into light.

By day the body is a lost address,
by night, heart-held and brain-pinned,

it unfolds you like a map or an empty shirt, and tells you this:

2.

It is hard to think of all the things you bury.
It is hard to be certain of what you have tried to forget.

Exile is a hard walk, an intricate tattoo.

It has finally grown into your face.

It has cut the apple, it has opened the fruit.

At night your blood sleeps in your clothes,
by day, the wrist

is a creation for the blind,
braille you touched on a stone once.

Over the river, gulls pick up the thermal
as they have done for years, angle,
and become a perfect brush-stroke.

What you have left is disallowed.
What you remember faithfully keeps time.

White dishes on the table.

3.

Years, keeping it all in mind.

For instance, the ache of snow, the patient rain
taking it all seriously.
The thrush breaking behind the house.

Outside, it is about to sleet, and in Bratislava,
half a life ago,
                    you cover your mouth and bite your fist,
and you still can't sleep it off.

Your hands smell of gasoline, you have been busy.
Or at night, when your body is the flat light of a star,

you lie in the dark alone, or not alone,

you get up past midnight and go where it is forbidden
and later, you spend the hours

among bushes, you are afraid to talk,
afraid to say a word.

You are simply afraid,

You are the road going right and left.
You are the knife and the fork.

You are the daily bread.

4.

Writing back in code, the word for home is August.
Yet the word for star, is simply star. The one guiding.

The unnamed one in a jury.

A cold calculation. Difficult instructions.

All winter we have been inventing a plot against the pear tree.
That really means we have thought of a return.

That really means we have come back.

Small chance.

We have received letters, and your kindness,
kisses, of course.

We have gone to hell.

This means we are well. This means we give you rest.

5.

Whatever was said is far below the grass now. The few odd verbs,
faces, eventually confined,
did nothing more than remain faces that once occurred.

The nights stood still, a blotter against our forgetting.

The river darkened to a stitch,
a phrase of music in the reeds.

But not the same river. And if music, then music
no longer our own.

Autumn again. It's quiet, but the storm rises, fruit swings
ripening on a branch.

To mind come those rooms, that society of theirs.
The wind weaves the same faces into memory.

Or else they rise, irrevocably, over the shrub,
and into the ledger.

Our bodies, white shirts blown into the fields.

THREE SONGS

—after three studies by Kathe Kollwitz

1.

Walls are leaning,
gathering something
from the wet earth.

A child strokes the mane of a horse
drinking long and hard after a run to nowhere.

Pain hits the windows hard—
inside, a woman slaps bread-dough on the table.

Two workers.
A man dies pruning a tree.

Outside, someone is sleeping so deeply
it looks as though he is about to speak.

2.

A string slapped the hands
between the knuckled fingers.

The seamstress fell asleep,
cloth in her hands.
The nakedness of the needle
holding a stitch of thread.

A roof fell silent
over someone
learning to speak
last words.

3.

In the distance, land
heaves with wind,

trees bolt upright
by the river.

Water is bitter to a tongue
ringing with song

about to end in a nearby grove.
Women carry

buckets of water to wash
battered clothes

longing for a body.

THE ROOM

—after a painting by Balthus

I could simply walk in some quiet Sunday and find nothing strange. It would be raining, and you would have just left the room filling with fragrance. I would sit, or stand. It no longer matters. The limbs stiffening in repose as they stretched to place a clean plate on a shelf, or open a door. The door. Outside, a blind leading a blind. It would be spring.

IMAGINING A SISTER

I can't imagine the photograph
standing upright on the table

eyes toward the light
hands folded together

as if in prayer
skirt pensively ironed

pattern ironed out
hair in a knot

to cover
a round shoulder—

the room smells of fruit
walls pull in to prevent

someone else from stretching
long heavy arms to touch

the tangles in your hair

MYTHOLOGY / FROM THE FRAGMENTS

Because a body moves from one empty house to another as though it
were a shirt, because in the mind the gardens are precisely detailed,
mapped, an entire peninsula often eerily lit, the province abandoned

because often even memory is neglected, erased, wiped clean, burned
out of existence, the door slammed shut, because the wall fills with
drawing, or becomes empty of drawing, because it becomes the wall

because it is no longer, because it is loved insanely, because it is looked for
in the eyes, in the hands, the gesture, a body no longer, no longer
the world, because it is inconsistent, a torch in the snow, an extinct
mythology

because in caricature longing remains the same, but without anesthetic,
because it becomes a gash, because it is a voice in a crowded theater, an
opera told to sit down, because it is asked, and is seated

because it is sung or kissed in absence, quieted and covered, whispered
to, because it is the one plate left empty, the one plate never filled,
because it is hunger, because in the empty notebook it is a score for voice

RESOLUTION

I am tired of arriving with the inch of snow each year.
I am tired of the finch warbling nonsense, as though he mattered.

All morning the body has made itself a long vowel,
and now, it is white keys, dark keys, instructed to type something into
memory.

Perhaps it is better to say something obscene, or shut up,
and leave it alone. Perhaps it is better to turn your back on it all.

All that bleeding was for nothing, repaired quickly.
The desire for ash was only the kindness of wind, its cruel passport.

This tongue, this hiss, is the sinister habit of speaking to the dead.
Ergo.

DUST

—to Wassily Kandinsky

A girl and her lover are scaling
an imaginary hill. In the distance, the sun

reflects from the surface of the lake:
trembling shadow of falling twilight.

In one of the houses a young woman
has fallen asleep on a couch, just so,

that her open shirt and breast
resemble the heart of the ticking

metronome on the mantle. Her fallen
arm, like the warped neck of a musical instrument

points to a bloated dog,
obliviously dead on its side.

And the dreams of old lovers, her father
floating over the chimney where she burns

the few postcards, past the thin
blue line of smoke rising

above the thin
horizontal line of trees.

The horses are asleep in their stalls
waiting for a fire that will drive them back.

But everything turns with the stars,
pales, darkens, and from the other side of the village

people in black
are returning from a funeral.

The night itself is still,
touches no one, except, from a distance,
and quite suddenly, a terrifying laughter
rises toward the moon.

And what becomes frightening is,
that I continue to look into this grave scene in the painting

and feel my bones resisting the dust
they will become in time.

I imagine the lovers are through with their love,
and they are dust themselves now,

as is the painter, who hallucinated
his way across the canvas in hope

that everything would remain precisely
as he wanted it to happen, though he

has long turned into the wind blowing
from the East, and I am not far behind.

A LATE AWAKENING

The sun comes in, defining everything in precise focus.

Where am I?

But does it really matter?

To my left, you are still asleep, the face of a deer etched into

your elbow.

Perhaps we have finally arrived.

Perhaps we arrived here by pure accident.

Is that why we are so inconsequent, leaning into each other's bodies?

But really, we must still be asleep, covered by the North wind, whose

body does not resemble ours.

It is snow.

It is snowing.

It is late November.

THE ARRIVAL

—after a photograph almost taken in Berlin

Wet slate roofs. Pigeons. A light.
A leaf on the sidewalk.
Shadows slipping between cobblestones.

It is already dusk
when you arrive from Paris,
smoke rising from the diesel
as you step out
with your black hair untied.

I am almost always
turning into that smoke,
into the pigeons landing
on the glass roof.

Or I wake up
and you come
with a shawl
black with stars.

NOCTURNE

Outside the house where you first raised
Your hand to the wood of a poem

The starlight mounted
Above the roof like a prayer

My mouth no longer speaks
My voice the wind has forgotten or lost

My hands the leaves
I return to
Old photographs
Black when I cup water in them

And place them to my lips
Quiet Inconsolable

Of a stranger coming to a ceremony
By the pond where no one has drowned

TO MAX JACOB IN THE BLUE

That man, pushed around in a wheelchair,
suddenly turned dark.

With the scratch of a fingernail, women
push in the folds of their lids
to give their eyes the look of statues.

There are nights that end in train stations.
There are train stations that end in nights.

———————

But I have dreamed long enough to forget you.

That sick, and dying,
through with walking, with going away,
you raised yourself a crack
to speak a few words.

How one night they beat you up,
and left you unconscious in a field
to witness the terrible silence your body would become.

How the leaves fell, soundlessly,
on Benoît-sur-Loire
                    for good, that autumn.

———————

When your eyes closed, they did not close on earth.

They closed on Christ, your Lord, in Picasso's rooms,

frightened, dying, one wing broken.

If your lips had anything to say about it
they would be the white shells of the stars
turning on in mid-sleep.

They would articulate the shadow of a hand
rising in speech, the guardian of voice.

———————————

In Drancy
everything was complicated
by your bum lungs,
and the interminable desire
to say no more,
to go out somewhere and bury it.
And if the mind is something to remember,
or to have remembered, as Augustine said,
then surely, you occur among us still,
but now, as the brother, the other,
the one leaning over a book,
underlining the blank passages.

———————————

To keep the hands busy,
the poet places to his forehead a glass of still water.

Listen to the boots . . .

Listen to the names . . .

A POEM IN YOUR NAME

—to the memory of Anne Frank

I.

At night, sometimes
when it's raining,
you appear, stone cold,
and place your hand
on a branch of a tree
where a name has been
knifed into the wood.

A train passes.
Birds rise
from the girders
of a bridge.

2.

A slow dawn. Swallows.
I walk out to the field
where the wheat
has just been cut,
looking for you,
a child pulled out of sleep
like a stone
lifted from a creek's edge.

The wheat is down, clods of damp earth—
haunted cradle of the newcomer.

3.

Horses far off.
Soldiers let them out
after setting their tails on fire.
They pass by the field,
frightened, crazed,
running toward Belsen.

I turn away and begin walking home.
It is March. By the lake
is a tree with a name
knifed into the bark.

THE LESSON

—after Günther Eich

This is the room.
And those are bells.

Those are poppies, and that was the field.
This is a hand, and that is a skull.

This is your face, and that is your mouth.
That is the tongue, and these are vowels.

That is a sound, and this is your hair.
Those are stars, those are oaks.

This is a window,
And that is the moon . . .

Brother to no one.

THINKING OF MY FATHER /
ON A BUS TO BALTIMORE

Before I can even look
the earth outside the window
becomes heavy.
This day
already filled with light
slants from a ditch.
80 miles from there
crows are knifed against the sky
rolling over the fields.

I suppose your steps
still make the sound of pigeons landing,
your brow is still creased, and perspiring,
your hands in your empty pockets.

How many thoughts circle a tired head
that you suddenly place in my lap
in a dream of your childhood.
The night around your shoulders,
you went to sleep and said nothing.

Nothing can be heard under the branches
of the tree where your father died
and returned in your dreams.

There are no sounds.
Not even of this match
I strike to see you better.

THE SUICIDE

Evening.
Hands
Heavy with darkness.

I wear the glasses
Of a murderer—
Making the earth
Silent and dark.

Like radium I have
My ghost, my shadow,

A horse,
His lungs,
His burning barn,

The moon
Which does not
Throw itself
Into the cellar,

Wind that does not sing
Of trees
And desperate snow . . .

A branch snaps
Where the fingers
Touched the trigger, taped,
Alone

PRAYER

It is so. It touches the clothes
with the rustle of leaves under a naked back.

And to sleep a little less now
is a small compassion.

That darkness you see, a land
of darkness, is darkness itself.

To be mad is to be like this.
Prayer is like this: to live on nothing.

Even I, the judicious failed scholar
find no reason for this.

Tomorrow, if I remember,
I will continue to repeat the same.

The way a face is pure.
The way fear is pure.

How simple it all becomes.
Thy deed is done.

DUET AFTER RAIN

On Brecht's grave a sparrow takes a drop of water from a leaf after rain.
A rainbow appears to the West.

I have no description, blood keeps time in my wrist

A light, delicate and calm as memory. Now, one can barely make out the
silhouettes riding over the lilac shrubs, Charon's uncomplicated boats
charting down the Spree.

Go out brief candle

Don't sleep alone simple grass. Bring the light which falls on the river, the
wind, morning opening into August.

It is almost dawn, but the sky is empty

While the photograph is developing, acids work on our faces. When they
grain into the sky, when they become invisible, hones, when all that's left
is a negative . . .

Abandoning everything, take refuge in me

While the photograph is developing . . .

THE JEWISH CEMETERY IN PRAGUE

It gets harder to walk
out of those crates which stop
light from entering.
The sky, bending over a body
touches the pale skin of grass
like the fevered head of a child.

You've left the town behind.
Trees long to lift you
gently from the splintered bed
into the wind. There is none.
It has stepped out of your bodies.

A MEDITATION ON LINES BY SANDOR CSOORI

I have done more than just walk along.
I have run away.

I should have ignored the pitchforks and lip-reading,
the henbones buried for luck,
the cold agonizing stares of the chairman of the institute.

I should have lain down in the mud
and listened to the tall elms speak my language,
the Danube, so elegantly slow, and months from freezing.

I should have asked the apples, I should have asked the pears.

I should have lied, I should have said this is not my name,
I should have forgotten them, ignored their uniforms.

I should have ignored my shirt, blood-stained and angry,
I should have dropped the rope.

—Are you listening?

Something is dying.
Something dies for good.

GAVRILO PRINCIP THINKS OF HIS HIGHNESS

A few words are enough even for the dead.

I have not been assassinated yet.

Simply put, I rose above myself.

It was still dawn.
It was still dark.

Impeccably dressed, it seems, the Sir in black has
      something to say.

Odd to hear it now.

And why should I ask for forgiveness?

They are burning the clothes of the dead beggars again.

It is early morning.
I have spread out my Sunday best over a chair.

But I know,
the Bosna is burning through my clothes, and my lover is
      still asleep.

To wake her now, I would have to be hungry and cold.

But I am almost happy.
Sarajevo is in my pocket.

COMING HOME

Sunday. Churchbells, You stood outside in a strange town, weary and cold, in a coat stolen from the Lost and Found. Steps on the pavement. Bags carried carefully as children. You pulled up the lapels of your coat and began walking toward the old church in the center of town. You could hear voices inside saying something softly in a language you did not know. Someone inside suddenly spoke your name, and you began walking away, frightened, toward the first doorway. I could hear you. You were breathing in my sleep eight thousand miles away.

You were breathing in my sleep. A moth was beating itself quiet against the panes. At night you lit a burned candle hours after the lights went out and sat at the window singing softly to yourself. Twenty-one years later, you come back with careful steps, no one's, the Ohio rising out of its banks. A few swallows. And the wind rocking them. Bells. You are alone.

A FIELD OF RED POPPIES

—in memory of M. Radnóti

I can see them now, I think, bowing against absence,
and trusting us.

They are, what my friend calls, a mind's glove.

Small death's head, small bodies that are not there.

It is all right to think of them in a photograph,
or in a dream.

It is all right that they assume their sinister bend.

What else can you say about poppies?

How they remind you of your childhood,
or of someone who is not there.

That's all.

And yet, this is a field

where they were throwing people once.

That's the story.

And it still matters. Because it is voiced.

RENE CHAR

Cure the bread. Set wine on the table. Hands are useless, they clay. Does it ever rain? You don't have to wake up anywhere. Fruit is blind. It's the tree that sees.

ANSWER

An itch of blood.

I have been translating my desire through a dozen
        languages.

In anger, I have stolen a star,
and replaced it with your thighs, which hinge open.

I have sucked blood from a fish.

. . . the dumb weight over my body,
the earth, with its slow grass and tall trees . . .

I have spoken to the emptiness above me.

Our arms are folded into wings.

Like Christ, we are flying somewhere.

I need you. I don't need you.

AFTERWARDS

August deep,
a thin line of grief swarms around the wild cherry.

The music coming on again.

It doesn't really matter where you are.
It doesn't really matter.

What can you say to that?

Simply, that you haven't arrived anywhere.
your destination, unknown.

Only then are you among the living.

FROM THE BESTIARY

—to the memory of Samuel Beckett and Thomas Bernhard

I.

. . . the architect throwing his hands into the fire, the faint inscription on the tongue

the invisible one, without wings, without shoes, calling out, slowing almost to a halt

summaries of dust recalled in redemption, music reconstructed ceaselessly

the garden full of light, a choir in itself

the fleck of green in a map remembered, the light strong

earth turned inward, a hand's gesture

repeated inadvertently, silently, the roses on the lattice falling into step with the black waltz

history, geography overtime, unapprehended, unpeopled

issued from the mildly insane

they are taking people away again, yes, they are taking people away

conducting a lucid conversation among themselves

one in which it is still dawn, in which it all goes on just the same, but a shade brighter the bloom, the flowers, the tulips, strictly alone, all that rowing

into a world in which the beloved are held up to the mind's light

birds in a crescendo, fruit in the bowl still

overlooked, the rain merciless, but welcome in the last chapter

probably overheard, raised octave by octave, ibid, angels despite
themselves, the door kicked open

I have to get the ceiling painted.

The ceiling of your skull, or the one above?

2.

VOICE:

. . . baroque almost in its futility, the knife-time, a stupefying reluctance
to understand, you heard it before, old kings dead flowerpots in windows,
small flags imperially hoisted, the circumstances making it previously
understandable, everyone is scared and quiet, write it down . . .

ANOTHER VOICE:

. . . a brief memory of summer, almost hallucinated, autumn stroking
downward, in the snows of this hemisphere, as someone has written, or is
soon to write, heart-mysteries in wheel-torture, the present state of affairs,
I told you this . . .

3.

. . . as if you were walking in snow. The rain standing at attention, gone mad in the past tense.

As if it were about to hide its face in your hands.

That darkness you see, a land of darkness, is darkness itself.

The earth, with its slow grass and tall trees, night, insufficiently night.

Ergo.

Without the darkness perhaps. Or imagine, one with all the lights in the guard towers off . . .

4.

. . . word, storm, ice, and field. Torches blazing in the webwork.

One thinks of lands, tangled, small houses, large silences

guarded by dogs

or the dogs removed, and someone always within earshot.

Counting the steps forward, counting the steps backward, the number remains the same . . .

5.

. . . years torn to seagulls above, the walls harden, grow soft, and harden
again

the ones who believed have prosed into dust, in principle, of course, it was
fixed

the hunchbacked oaf observed from above, braying endlessly with each
turn

a grand spectacle, applause rose with each blow of the skull against the
enclosure

countless maps stabbed into the walls, also found later, a frightening
portrait of God . . .

6.

. . . ugly perhaps. But the few moments of kindness, are kindness
themselves

a strange inflection of what continues, a strange place, where one begs
and laughs.

Even the dogs have become friendly.

Odd, how they lick your hands now, or nip the skin around the knuckle.

Terrible beasts following unseen . . .

II

FRAGMENTS & ABANDONED VERSE

LAMENT

Distant music
outside the window.
Darkness too
in my reflection.
Beneath the bending
of sounds,
I rise half-woken.
Only your dead mother
is standing outside,
the one who swam out
too far
and left you holding
a pebble the size
of a child's head.
I turn back
as if I had suddenly
decided to walk past
the room on Morgan Street
where her empty clothes are kept,
the walls
where your solitude
hangs from one of her hairs.

I observe
the process of recognition.
I am not the one
to pull her out
by her wet hair
and hand her to you
the way a child is handed
her first toy.

I am here, there.
She too is there

hiding in the corner
of your eye
suddenly too wet
to remember

AUTUMN 1979, BROOKLYN

Exhausted sleep. 3 o'clock in the morning.
I lean over you in the darkness
to whisper something into your dream.

As a child you moved through these streets
among the strange languages of shopkeepers,
the vague steps of mothers pushing their carriages.
It was raining then as it is now,
the drops hitting the sidewalk
like the minnows I had once caught barehanded,
that I dropped on the driest brookstones.
Only the night outside. Shadows of streetlamps
quietly slipping into doorways.

You were sleeping then, dreaming. You are
dreaming this now. In sleep you find
that sureness which one finds
walking into an empty room
smelling of wet grass and sweat.
When you suddenly turn
the room will be filled
with a clean light,
the light from the last
motion of the hands
raised toward the stars.

A PHOTOGRAPH OF US

—after a photograph by Lori Reidel

Late Summer. A slight breeze coming in
from the park. The morning light
quieting itself past the long curtains
to my right, past the table, to a small
deathmask of your face, a child's.

It must be terrible to be condemned
so early, to darkness, secrecy,
a stillness we carry in our pockets,
like stones, but simpler.

I speak of your face now, turned away
from its own, even though darkness
has taken your body, and you will never
own your hands.

Blame the night.
Blame its phrases.

You are in sleep, in water, face, stone,
and the day darkens.

Wind, be kind to her.

ROMANZA ANDALUZA
—to her

Tonight, I thought of
the line of children,
like music,
widening from the school for the blind
in Málaga.
How the practice of their love in the dark
is precise, and tuned
like reeds in wind,
or a mosquito's thin pitch.
How the darkness
is so absolute,
that it hides
in the purity and beauty
of a human face.

And you would have to listen to the grass
for a long time
to hear their silence . . .

All that is in the body,
which is yours now,
asleep.
Your beautiful face rises from my memory,
infoliating.
I accept this blessing,
this loneliness of hours,
this bereaved lament of metronomes.

I throw my arm
around your absence.

The mortality of things
is so abrupt,
that it rises like a body
out of calm water.
But I will stop.

I can already see this love poem
is nothing to show you.
It is pure,
like the ring of a small bell.
Like a sudden waking chime,
it is definite.
Tonight, I lift
a quiet glass of wine to my lips,
and leave the dark house
where we have lived.

THINKING ABOUT A HOLOCAUST VICTIM

A cold rain. Workmen cursing
the clouds, and then rain.
A cold quiet rain.

Before they knocked on your door
you packed your last belongings
and came here to sit at dusk.
You were singing your mother's song.
Quietly, just for yourself.

I stop the car
by the deep lake
where you had to hide underwater,
the thin straw to your mouth.
They never found you,
you hid so deep. Deep as a stone.

Now in the twilight I begin
turning over the pebbles of the shore.
A small crayfish backs away
toward the deep where you are.
It is so quiet
even my footsteps seem different.
And your breath is still
underwater.

THE TRIBES

Birds overhead
pass South.
Fields of battered corn
flat under the snow.
Trucks howl and downshift along 95.
It was here I thought I saw you:
brother, father, pain,
ravens in the snow,
whistling peacocks of my childhood.

The first time
I came to this empty field
I was telling myself
I am that hymn
the wind keeps singing to itself.
My ribs swelling and grating,
I too began to sing,
crowing without a nest.

Winter, and I return
to the same stubble-field.
There was frost last night
I am told by a beer-stumbling
hunter who slept in the crotch
of a tree all night
and damn near froze.

He motions to me,
offering bourbon
and I oblige.
He asks me
if I like rabbit
and I say no. He passes
a smile and gives me more drink
picking his rabbit up
by the cold ears
and strutting away cold
and miserable all for the sport.

His wife must be waiting
in their trailer-home
recognizing the grey morning.
He will be there soon,
to her warm breast. If I lit
a cigarette, I would be like him,
swaggering home
over the hammered earth
under the birds
heading South.

REQUIEM

I lie in the dark
trying to remember.

I still smell
the fresh painted
walls in the house
I lived in, the man
upstairs, drunk,
kicking his dog,
the woman next
door yelling at
the moon out of
pain in her bones.

They are not here,
the two, waking
me up every
morning. Even

in sleep there are
long hallways where
no one can
look at the lives
we led, or the
singing we lost,
the building where
a woman jumped
from the fourth floor
window and I was
sleeping too hard

to hear the sirens
come and take her
with their stars,
the coma that
came later when
I left, when she
could no longer
hear me on the
stair, coughing
into my sleeve.

You are three voices
singing in me.
Growing. You have
come to sing
Hosanna in
your accents.
I am among you
singing. We
are growing
into words.

BEARING

Overhead, chevron birds gave direction.
Despite everything, our lives went there.

There was a verb that would take
decades to learn.

Brother, will I go grey now, without you?
Years ago, a boy opened a small blade

and knifed into treebark
his name to outlive him.

A SMALL CEREMONY

When I close my eyes before sleeping
they are there. And when

you turn over, they're
somewhere by the Hudson,
because that is where

I placed them. Small,
antiquated women,
dressed in black.

If I fell asleep,
I would be
on the other side

of the river.
And if I could see them,
I would remember

my childhood.
They would be coming
with baskets and axes,

careful, where thin
ice separates.

I dreamed this often
when I was young. But
because I was a boy,

I did not know the hands
which shaped the hole in the ice.
The same hands kneaded bread,

spread washed sheets
over the ice, to dry,
and they would freeze into glass.

And if any of those women
are still alive, I would
like to thank them. Because

they have remained in their
beauty. Because I can still
see them. When I close my eyes,
the world is a room, growing dark.

BALLADE

—again for Frank Stanford

Strange,
        how you arrive
                with no address in mind.

Thistles
        lift in wind. You are asleep,
                or dozing.

It is late autumn,
        late dusk; fields
                compare their notes,

And even in Ohio,
        in the dark house,
                one light burning.

You are asleep,
        or dozing, holding
                your sex as though

There was nothing left;
        a lover's clay hand, perhaps,
                a glass of quiet wine,

Your hands,
        which suddenly fall,
                one after the other,

Like leaves,
            but less perfect,
                        and you being to prose.

And all the things
            that are cruel:
                        the folding of wings,

The vernacular of grass,
            and the whiteness of wrists,
                        disappear in speech.

Now, and just
            for a moment,
                        I live myself into this,

Into all that is mine,
            then slowly turn away
                        and vanish.

PAVESE, A DEPARTURE, A ROMANCE

Of course the emptiness of the room doesn't
matter. As usual a warm rain is falling.

Of course, the emptiness doesn't matter now,
outside of Lorain, Ohio. The darkness is
like a shirt filling with a body that was
carried out of the hotel in Turin, in 1950.

And again, a quiet Sunday.

When I look into an empty room, I feel the dust
in my clothes quicken, and my shoes grow large.
But I turn my face away.

Pressed against yours, it becomes quiet, finally,
like a forgotten instrument. It is calm now,
as we sleep, and when rising, I will remember
all the years.

All would be well. All would be lovely. If the
damned would only stay damned.

A FRAGMENT AFTER ROBERT DESNOS

Today, because of you, I can walk
under the same beaten sky, speak
to the same wind.
      Or the placing of hands
on a girl's waist
becomes holy, the way stilling trees
are suddenly silenced.

I can ask for nothing more.

Today, my voice will calm,
and until the brush stops breaking
behind the house, I will dream
fiercely of you, I will demand everything
of silence.

And today, because of you,
all your self,
I say nothing, I say
I am not myself now,
or I say, "We have drunk this silence,
Lord." Or I say nothing again.

Because of you today,
because of you,
it is sad to become earth
eventually, the sad lepidoptera,
with its last open wings.

But sensibility demands another.

Today, because of you,
and because of you,
I ask the sea nothing,
ask nothing.

A LITTLE MUSIC

It begins like a sentence.
Like silence.
A line of music rising
like a hand in speech.
It begins, for instance, here,
among the grass
and the light.
It begins with a name,
your name,
even though you cannot hear it,
or afford it now,
though you swear by it.

In this dream
you are still nothing, or wind.
For days, you sit by a piano
listening to the notes
it types into your memory.
Then you become shadow,
hovering over a sleeper's body.
To rest, you light on the lips.
You will not be rebuked.

Strange, how even you
keep singing to yourself . . .
It is dark,
and the wind leans into you.
It suddenly occurs to you
that you are alone,
and have no place to go.

DEMONOLOGY

apples falling all night in the orchard. Instead
of flowers, your face kissed like an apple.
Instead of apples, fear kissed from your face
like a stone's throw

in translation.

DECEMBER 1992

We were speaking with the other, with the echo of the other. He was stitching something horrible together, something far darker than even our forefathers could imagine. An entire world, it seems, with the light off.

PROVERBS (OF THE SEAS?)

There is thimbleful of kindness in this whorl of a black rose.

Inside are meadows, lashing seas, rivers broken out of recognition.

Your face inside, in troubled, asleep.

Why is it that

THE WORLD WITHIN A LOST GLOVE

Dreaming of home is a cruel joke. In the dim house, an impression of solitude, or of a garden abandoned. A picture of ordered emptiness. Intelligence erased.

By the river, a short blind man, without a dog, is leading a tall blind man without a cane. The two are followed by a nurse pushing a wheelchair. She is wearing sunglasses, and her stockings are torn.

The weatherman predicts darkness for the evening. The weather's history. Accidents. The strategies doubtful.

In a dark stone, once, you were whole, an insurmountable ship that once plowed the world.

UNTITLED FRAGMENT

And then came storms that lashed the sea.
The book became the book, and the children kept on playing.

Inspired by actual events, a rope of sand remained a rope of sand.
Out of waters sewn by Satan

Words reduced to moments. Moments translated into words.

NOTES

Between your breasts there is a space so small that
         all maps are
reduced to a whisper

The heart is an invisible shepherd guided by the
         silence of a vast
continent

It counts the beats of wind in fields of snow

Or holds the mind's light to a face endeared long
         ago

Principium et finis almost a pitcher of flowers

There are no hours in this landscape. At times, white
         hands pass
over the surface of this surface, and when they are
         finished, they
begin all over again

The voices are usually twofold, building a small
         flame in memory

Indexing lives and offering asylum between the vast
         kilometers of
the dead

There are no hours in this landscape

BREAD FOR ANOTHER DAY

Between your breasts there is a space so small that all maps
are reduced to a whisper.
The heart is an invisible shepherd guided by the silence of a
vast continent.
It counts the beats of wind in fields of snow
or holds the mind's light to a face endeared years ago.

Apples falling all night in the orchard.
Instead of flowers, your face kissed like an apple.
Instead of apples, fear kissed from your face like a pebble's
                throw in translation,
the sound itself almost a torso.

White hands pass over the surface of this surface, and when
                they come to the end
they open and begin again
forming this landscape,
which is without time or asylum between the vast
                kilometers of the dead.

This is a voice which you have heard before, but now it is
                higher, worlds brighter.
Throw a coat over your cold body.
Throw a coat over your cold body.

YOUR SLEEP, ENDYMION

I.

Even though I am not dead,
I lean over you in the darkness.
I am not the phantom
that comes to children at dawn,
though I've seen him hiding
in a long beam of light,
which will be touching you soon.
Neither am I the hungry man

who will rattle the garbage can
outside and move on,
or the lonely woman, who throws away
three dying roses. No, I am

someone you left, someone who
slept next to you. I held you
even after there was nothing left,
the way I held the petals
of the dying roses together.
Your soul too, brittle as cocaine.

2.

If I could, I would tell you
how I hated silence, because
that's where you were. I could
tell you many things, but you
would not want to remember,

as you do not now, that faint
twitch as you realize the sounds
across the street are noises
coming from the school for the blind
rehearsing for the annual dance.

3.

And when they hold each other,
skating over the floor,
which is the color of bone,
I can make any mythological
connection. I can say that
when they grow, and look in each
other's eyes behind a tree in a park,
she will stare through him at the sky,
and he through her, into the grass.

4.

Years before, one light is left on
to remind the gods they are sleeping.

And when night comes, and they
do not rise,
the rooms will be dark.

I remember someone weaving
a sleeping figure into the stars.

A DREAM OF MY DEATH

—a poem ending in a line by John Berryman

In the end, it doesn't matter.
You grow dark,
and I step out of the body

I have washed for years.
It is not difficult.

But now, a button is gone,
a cuff is stained.

Hinges of the body
come to rust,

and I will forget.

I will forget the beauty of a face,
of a girl's legs in dry leaves.

I will forget my right,
and let my left remember.

And this is about silences now.
Not even the thin diction of a mosquito
can enter it.

How dark it is . . .
No one has the stones.

O, yes, the stones . . .

Night within me
Night without me

I come your child to you

THE HAND

It is really a map. Or rather, whatever is left
after it's been skinned.

You can trace the whorls in the flesh, which bloom,
unpredictably, like a fingerprint in the mind's shadow.

Or staring at it, it suddenly occurs to you,
that it belongs to a murderer.

What is left, is left.

What it knows . . . What it doesn't know

ACKNOWLEDGMENTS

Grateful acknowledgments are made to the following magazines and anthologies in which some of these poems appeared:

Artist's Pulp, The Boundaries of Twilight: An Anthology of Czechoslovak-American Writing, Cincinnati Poetry Review, Columbia, Contemporary East European Poetry (Ann Arbor: Ardis, 1983), *The Graham House Review, Open Places: American Writers Abroad, Poetry International, Pleiades, Provincetown Arts, Salmagundi,* and *Shankpainter.*

Note: "Homage to Georg Trakl," "To Max Jacob in the Blue," and "René Char" intentionally include lines taken from these poets.

Svetozar Daniel Simko was born in Bratislava in 1959, and emigrated with his family following the Warsaw Pact invasion of Czechoslovakia in 1968. He was educated at Oberlin College and earned a Master of Fine Arts at Columbia University and a Master of Library Science at Pratt Institute in New York. In 1986, he was awarded a fellowship at the Fine Arts Work Center in Provincetown. His translation of Georg Trakl, *Autumn Sonata*, received the Poet's House Translation Prize and was published by Moyer-Bell, Ltd. in 1988 and 1998. His own poetry has been translated into Czech, Slovak and German, and a collection entitled *Svet V Stratenej Rukavci* (*The World Within a Lost Glove*) was published posthumously in Bratislava. He worked as a librarian at the New York Public Library until his death in 2004.

Carolyn Forché is Lannan Professor of Poetry at Georgetown University. Her most recent books include *The Angel of History* and *Blue Hour*.

James Reidel is a poet, translator, editor, and biographer. His forthcoming projects include *Love Is Like Park Avenue: The Fiction of Alvin Levin* (New Directions), with John Ashbery, and *A Pale Blue Lady's Hand* (Godine), a novel by Franz Werfel.